Introduction

There was a time when steam road vehicles were so much a part of the scene in B[...] of notice at their passing along the way, whether in town or in the countryside. Stea[...] daily life, much as tractors, vans or articulated lorries are a common sight on our road[...] the length and breadth of Britain steam wagons, perhaps by Foden or Sentinel went about their workaday tasks. Light haulage might also be in the capable hands of steam tractors, often to be seen with a couple of pantechnicons behind the drawbar, moving some ones furniture from house to house. Heavy haulage was the province of the big boys - the Road Locomotives - impressively powerful machines by Burrell, Fowler or perhaps Garratt or McLaren. For many years, even after steam had disappeared from other spheres, these beautiful engines continued to dominate the haulage of heavy industrial loads, simply because they were the only vehicles powerful enough to do the job economically.

All these steamers also appeared in the countryside, where the tractors were also to be seen hauling timber from the woodlands to sawmills. Villagers were well accustomed to the seasonal travels of the threshing contractors with their Burrells or Claytons pulling drum, elevator and perhaps even a living van for the crew if they were away from home. Likewise, in the parts of England where larger fields made their use economical, the ploughing teams would travel between jobs - a pair of engines with plough or cultivator, van and water dandy; in season, the ring of a Fowlers gears would signal the approach of a team long before the smoke appeared over the hedgerows.

Great excitement was caused by the arrival of the fair, itself with its attendant engines, in many ways perhaps the prime donnas of the steam world. Yet these smartly turned out locomotives and tractors were probably among the hardest worked of all, covering many thousands of miles on their seasonal circuit; nor did they rest off the road as they provided the electricity to power the fair for the duration of its stay.

In complete contrast, the most humble, yet paradoxically perhaps the best known was the steam roller, which made and maintained the 'rolling roads of Britain'. These machines were so much part of the scene that even today their modern diesel counterparts are still sometimes called 'steam rollers'! Perhaps the fact that their work was done in full sight of the world at large, or that they tended to stay in a particular area for some time may account for their being so well remembered. They were also the last type of steam engine to work the roads of Britain commercially, some even surviving until the late seventies; many people associate the rampant horse emblem of Aveling and Porter with steam rollers - not surprisingly in view of the numbers that they built.

Gradually, over a period of time, steam disappeared from our roads. Fortunately, the efforts of the preservationists, starting in the early fifties ensured that considerable numbers of engines have survived for our enjoyment. Fortunately also there have always been engine owners who have enjoyed driving their charges to and from rallies; an increasing number of clubs and organisations include road runs as a part of their show. Planning either a journey or a road run with steam has to be done carefully with modern traffic in mind. Difficult or bust routes must be avoided and, of course such things as the availability of water must be considered. There are few better sights and sounds than steam engines on the road; the fact that the routes chosen for their journeys usually involve the quieter roads and lanes of the countryside merely adds to the photographic potential. All but two of the photographs in this book have been taken of steam engines on road runs or travelling to and from rallies; I am most grateful to the engine owners for letting me know their plans, and to rally organisers who have put on road runs. I hope that they, and all readers will enjoy reliving this memory of days of steam on the road.

Above: Heading home from a rally at Cricket St Thomas in Somerset is Sentinel DG4 waggon No. 8393, built in 1930. It is now owned and maintained by the crew of HMS Sultan, a Navy establishment at Gosport, as a voluntary recreational activity. The DG series Sentinel came between the 'Super' and 'S' models. 'DG' denotes 'Double Geared' units and both four ('DG4') and six ('DG6') wheeled versions survive in preservation.

1. Clayton and Shuttleworth 7NHP traction engine No. 48224, 'Valiant' was built in 1919 and spent most of its time in East Anglia. In 1985, it was purchased by Ron Sams of Taunton, who is seen on the last lap of his journey from a local rally in 1986. Note the extra plates fitted between the rear wheel strakes to improve the ride on metalled roads; an unsparing engine with steel wheels is not the most comfortable transport!

2. By chance 'Valiant's' sister engine, No. 48225, 'Dominator', was already in the Taunton area, having been owned for many years by Cyril Thomas of West Buckland. The twins were first reunited at a local rally in May 1986 and have appeared together on a number of occasions since. Crewed by Maurice Lewis and Dennis Toogood, No. 48225 is seen at Shoreditch near Taunton homeward bound from Taunton Agricultural Show in August 1990.

3. Survivors of the engines built by William Allchin Limited in Northampton are not particularly numerous. Here one of the older examples is seen on a road run, crossing Queen Square, in Bristol. No. 1261 is a 8NHP single cylinder machine, built in 1903, and has been owned by the Henton family since new.

4. 'Lady Diana' is a 6NHP single cylinder engine built in Ipswich in 1904 as No. 15609 by Ransomes, Sims and Jefferies. Like the Allchin above she is seen on a Bristol road run. Originally supplied with steel-shod wheels, 'Lady Diana' has been fitted with rubber tyres for road work.

5. *Many manufacturers of steam engines produced small tractors. These were fast. easily handled and could legally be driven on the road by one man. Wallis and Steevens of Basingstoke encased the motion work of their later tractors in an oil filled casing - hence the legend 'Oilbath Tractor' on the canopy sides of No. 7289, 'Tinkerbell'. Built in 1912, this little engine had just changed hands when photographed below the M5 motorway in Devon.*

6. *'Tinkerbell' is a twin cylinder, compound engine, rated at 4NHP and weighing about five tons. Here we have an example of an earlier, single cylinder Wallis and Steevens tractor, without the oilbath system, or the extra 'belly tanks' for water. 'Goliath' is owned - and here driven - by Giles Romanes, and is a well known sight on our rally fields. Its serial number and early history are unknown, but it was built in 1902.*

7.   Apart form a glimpse of a modern car wheel in the background, this photograph might well have been taken in the heyday of working steam. In fact Ransomes Sims and Jefferies 4NHP compound tractor no. 36220 was photographed being driven through Taunton by owner Bill Scurlock, soon after restoration in August 1988. Built in 1920, it was, for some years the makers' show engine.   It visited many shows, with a new serial number each year; it is believed to have carried no fewer than seven numbers before sale in 1926.

8.   Taskers of Andover were also manufacturers of small tractors.   Their 'Little Giant' of Class 82 was a 4NHP compound machine, unusual in that the final drive was by roller chain rather than the gear trains favoured by other makers. 'Wee Tam', No. 1697 was built in 1916.

9. In the autumn of 1907, the RAC held a series of trials for commercial vehicles. Charles Burrell and Sons Limited of Thetford won an award for their 5 ton steam tractor. Subsequently, this compound design became known as their 'Gold Medal' tractor, and a number have survived in preservation. One very original example is No. 3245 (built in 1910) owned by John Cooper; it usually travels to rallies under its own steam. Here it climbs homewards up to the Blackdown Hills south of Taunton; a stirring sight, the sound effects were even better!

10. Burrell 'Gold Medal' tractors were also popular with showmen. A widely rallied example is the beautifully maintained No. 3192, 'St. Bernard' owned by James Gilbey. Built in 1910 as a crane engine for the War Department it was later used by showman J H Herbert of Southampton. In this view, Mr and Mrs Gilbey must be glad of 'St. Bernard's' canopy as they brave the rain in the centre of Bristol, followed by Sentinel 'Super' waggon No. 8109.

11. *A growing number of small gatherings of steam vehicles take place during the winter months. One such is the Somerset Traction Engine Club's Taunton Road Run, instituted during the Christmas period in 1988. Local owner Ron Sams, now the proud owner of Aveling and Porter single cylinder tractor No. 10563, braves the cold during the 1989 event. No. 10563, 'Old Peculier' began life as a six ton roller in Gloucestershire.*

12. *Aveling and Porter tractors were another make popular with showmen. No. 7612 'Amelia' was built in 1912 as a haulage tractor, with compound cylinders and rated at 4NHP. Showman's tractor fittings were added in preservation. Note the very distinctive design of cast wheels, a feature of Aveling tractors in contrast to the more common style of fabricated steel wheel.*

13. Len Crane's Fowler Road Locomotive is a well known exhibit at rallies and road runs both in Britain and on the continent. This fine crane locomotive was built in 1929, to Class 86; no. 17212 is a compound of 8NHP, and tips the scales at around the 21 ton mark. Supplied to John Thompson, the Wolverhampton boilermakers, this beautiful engine is seen enjoying a break during the 1987 Bristol Road Run. In this view the drive to the crane's winding drum can be clearly seen.

14. Who could wish for a better mode of wedding transport? In May 1987, a young couple at Street in Somerset emerged from the church to find this entourage waiting to convey them to their reception. The engine is 1918 Ruston Proctor No. 52266, 'Corn Maiden', owned and driven by Brian Wilkins; behind is a typical Somerset farm wagon. Better than any limousine!

15. An engine named 'Ikanopit' is clearly capable of showing others a clean pair of heels - or wheels! Foster 'Wellington' 4NHP compound tractor No. 14608 was built in 1930; it will be noticed that full electric lighting, powered by a steam generator is fitted. This little engine travels many miles under its own power every year to rallies in many areas.

16. *Brollies in Bristol 1: Weather conditions for the Bristol Road Run seems to alternate annually between very wet and very dry! In 1986, Richard Sandercock drives his well known 5NHP Burrell compound Road Locomotive No. 3996 'Conqueror', of 1924 vintage, through the centre of the city; passengers in the traction wagon shelter under a variety of umbrellas.*

17. *Brollies in Bristol 2: In 1988, the traction wagon travels behind Jack Miles's 6NHP Burrell Showman's Road Locomotive, No. 3090, 'Fermoy'. Built in 1909 for the Midlands showmen Pool and Bosco, like many of their kind she later spent many years threshing. She has been owned by the Miles family since 1969. Like the Foster tractor in plate 15, 'Fermoy' has electric lighting fitted.*

18. *Brollies in Bristol 3: A single brolly this time! Sentinel 'Super' waggon No. 8109 was built in 1929 and first owned by the local operator whose name she now carries. An 'undertype' waggon, she has the engine between the frames, with boiler and firebox in the cab. The distinctive style of wheels fitted by this builder will be noted.*

19. *Fine weather in Bristol! Making rapid progress along Anchor Road are Andrew Melrose and Charles Daniel's handsome Burrell Road locomotive No. 3937 'Janet', built in 1922. This 6NHP engine, which began its working life in Scotland, is one of the maker's 'single crank compounds; in this design, both pistons drive a common crank. The majority of compound machines have two cranks and sets of motion. Single crank road locomotives are not as common as their double crank sisters.*

20. *Road steam power at its best: two Burrells, No. 3159 'Gladiator' and No. 3937 'Janet' join forces to haul a heavy boiler in Cornwall. With clear exhausts and superb sound effects they pound up 1 in 6 of Engine Hill, near Porthtowan during the 1990 St. Ages Road Run. 'Gladiator' is possibly one of the Duchy's best known engines. Originally owned by Anderton and Rowland, this 7NHP showman's road locomotive was, in 1990, running without showland fittings pending completion of its restoration; when the work is finished, it will revert to its full showman's guise.*

21. *Later in the day, the pair are seen descending the switchback Gover Hill while returning to the rally field. Handbrakes are being applied to control the load, in this case a Cornish boiler built in 1900 by Holman Bros. of Camborne. It was on its way, via the St. Agnes Rally, from St. Austell to the Trevithick Society's Levant Mine project.*

22. Hill climbing in another part of the country. The immaculate Ruston Proctor 5NHP single cylinder traction engine No. 52266, 'Corn Maiden', climbs towards Somerton in Somerset, with older sister No. 51737 in tow. Both engines had attended the South Somerset Agricultural Preservation Club's 1986 'Yesterday's farming' event, and No. 51737 owned by George Train was heading for restoration - a project nearing completion at the time of writing.

23. A remarkably similar scene in East Anglia. Colin Pigott drives his 1907 Fowell 7NHP traction engine uphill from Baldock, heading for a real ale festival at the neighbouring village of Wallington. Only seven of the engines built by the St. Ives company survive and No. 93 'The Abbot' is one of five 7NHP singles; the other two are 8NHP machines.

24. Rural Rollers 1: High on the Blackdown Hills of Somerset close to the Devon border, Aveling and Porter 8 ton piston valve single cylinder roller No. 10590 heads past Holmore Cross while on its way to the 1986 Honiton Hill Rally. Just appearing in the background is fellow traveller and sister engine No. .9128 'Major'. No. 10590 was built in 1923.

25. Rural Rollers 2: A scene which really evokes memories of the past as Robert Crabbe drives his ten ton Fowler Class DNB compound roller and living van along the lanes of South Somerset. No. 17501, built in 1927 was one of a number fitted with Fowler-Woods tar spraying gear. The large belly tanks held the tar; with spraying gear at the rear and a chipping hopper in tow, a contractor had a self contained resurfacing machine. Nowadays 'Pentland Queen's' tanks hold additional water - very useful on a road run.

26. Rural Rollers 3: Aveling and Porter twelve ton single No. 9128 'Major', built in 1920 photographed, with water cart in tow, at Norton Fitzwarren near Taunton in 1986, while travelling between rallies. Originally operated by Staffordshire County Council, she was, in 1986, owned by Cyril Finch; she is seen pulling away from a hilltop pause to check fire and water level.

27. Rural Rollers 4: Making steady progress up Engine Hill in Cornwall is Burrell No. 4041, a ten ton single built in 1926. When new she went to William Elworthy of Tiverton, Devon, and later worked for the well known Cornish contractors, R. Dingle and Sons of Stokeclimsland.   Following preservation in different parts of England, she returned to her old haunts in 1989.

28. *A scene from the 1990 Taunton Road Run. Dave and Robert Allen drive their fine Clayton and Shuttleworth roller up to the Tone bridge in the centre of Taunton. Built in 1923 No. 48751 spent its working life with Messrs. W W Buncombe of Highbridge who operated a number of Clayton rollers. Following behind is Burrell No. 3245 (see page 6)*

Plate 1. Leaving Bishop's Lydeard for home after a steam gathering at the West Somerset Railway is Clayton and Shuttleworth 7NHP single cylinder traction engine no. 48224 'Valiant'. Built in 1919, this fine engine spent its working life and early preservation years in East Anglia: it moved to Somerset about a year before this May 1986 photograph was taken.

Plate 2. Colin Wait drives his immaculate 1916 Fowler K7 ploughing engine to the start of the 1984 Bristol Docks Rally Road Run. No. 14256 'General French' a 16NHP compound, was restored by Colin, though many considered that it was well beyond rescue. At the time of writing, Colin is well on the way to finishing the restoration of an even more derelict Foden wagon.

Plate 3. Aveling and Porter Showmans tractor No. 7589 'Princess Victoria', waits for crew at the end of the 1984 Bristol Road Run. Built in 1914 this 4NHP compound tractor worked for both Kent and Huntingdon County Councils. Showmans fittings were added in preservation. The very fine rampant horse, the Aveling trade mark, and arms of the County of Kent, will be noted.

Plate 4. Foden 'C' type tractor No. 13484 'Talisman', built in 1930, and photographed at the 1984 Bristol Dock Road Run. Fitted with a winch and converted to pneumatic tyres, this is a particularly well presented example.

Plate 5. With a strong following wind bending the willows in the background Ruston Proctor 5NHP single No. 52266 'Corn Maiden' makes swift progress across the Somerset levels. It took me a long time to locate 'Corn Maiden' and her crew on this occasion. With no real knowledge of their route, listening from the roadside was a fruitless exercise; a level road and rubber tyres meant that she was travelling very quietly while the wind carried away what little noise she made. We eventually came upon them more by luck than planning. A roller or ploughing engine would have been much easier to find!

Plate 6. Aveling and Porter ten ton single cylinder roller No. 5124 (of 1902) traverses Baldwin Street in central Bristol during the 1990 road run through the city streets. Owned by Ford Bros., the Cheddar contractors, this is another engine from the Buncombe fleet.

Plate 7. Threading the main street at Gillingham Dorset during the carnival parade is Marshall Road locomotive No. 57304 'Challenger'. Built in 1911 this 7NHP engine is a compound with overhead slide valves. It is towing what must be the most unusual, not to say the largest, living van on the rally scene. An ex. BR brake van on road chassis, it is owned by Dave Antell. 'Challenger' is believed to be the only 7NHP, 3 speed Marshall in preservation.

Plate 8. About to set off as the first of a number of steam entries in the 1990 Gillingham (Dorset) carnival is Mike Ford with his 1924 Aveling roller.   Originally in the Dingle fleet in Cornwall, No. 10981 'Penare' is an 'E' class twelve ton machine.

29. *Classic proportions! The crew of Aveling and Porter ten ton 'E' Class roller are clearly eager to restart their Bristol run after the lunch break. This well restored engine (No. 10555 of 1923) was also a part of the Buncombe fleet, being sold later to Paignton RDC.*

30. *Returning to its old home in Bishop's Lydeard is Burrell roller No. 4004 'Pride of Somerset'. After many years in the fleet of W J King this attractive eight ton roller was sold in 1970. Owners Arthur and Richard Bridge bought her in 1977 and restored her to the fine condition seen here. In the picture she is seen on her way to be photographed at the King's yard while attending a rally at the West Somerset Railway in August 1990; nowadays her home is in Cheshire.*

31. *Taunton Road Run 1989; Aveling and Porter twelve ton single No. 10981 'Penare', with owner Mike Ford in charge, and Dave Allen steering, waits at traffic lights; following is Nick Baker with his fine Burrell 7NHP traction engine No. 4049, 'Daphne'. 'Penare' a 1924 'E' Class roller is another ex-Dingle's engine.*

32. *Only four of the rollers constructed by Thomas Green of Leeds are believed to exist in Britain. One of these is No. 1968, 'Rose', eight tons, and built in 1917. This neat little roller is one of a number still owned by Devon County Council, and in the care of custodians. Clarence de la Cour has no. 1968. When photographed in August 1960, she was in the final stages of overhaul; cladding sheets had not been refitted so that the wooden insulation was visible on the boiler.*

33. *Driving an engine with no canopy is very pleasant in fine weather; heavy rain is a different matter and the expressions on the faces of the crew of this Aveling sum up their feelings! No. 5467 built in 1904, started its life with Croydon RDC; later it was with W W Buncombe. When photographed it was owned by Tony Beeching, who is at the regulator.*

34. *Ploughing engines were once a common sight on the rural roads of some parts in Britain. Their size and speed makes them something of a handful in modern traffic, but the 1990 St. Agnes Road Run gave spectators the impressive sight of two machines in action, both from the Daniel Brother's stable. Fowler BB1 class No. 15163 was in the capable hands of Dave and Robert Allen, having a change from their Clayton roller; Dave and his brother are restoring a pair of similar Fowlers.*

35. *Also on the run was Daniel Brothers' other ploughing engine, McLaren No. 1552 'Hero'. Only two of the ploughers constructed by this Company have survived into preservation, the other being No. 1541 'Avis'. Built in 1919, 'Hero' is a 16NHP compound, weighing some 22 tons. In contrast, Fowler No. 15163, while also of 16NHP, is somewhat lighter at about 17 tons.*

36. *A rarity seen on the 1988 Bristol road run was this 1933 Marshall tandem vertical boilered roller. Owned and restored by Andrew Melrose, No. 87125 is the sole British survivor of only seven built to this design. Equipped with power steering (steam operated) and instant reverse, this machine was of a generation specifically designed for rolling tarmacadam, where stopping on the soft surface left pronounced hollows. It will be seen that the firedoor is on the side of the firebox; boiler manhole covers are also prominent.*

37. *The above photograph shows No. 87125 before restoration was complete. Though the shot below was not taken on the road, but at Langport Rally in 1989. I have included it, in fairness to Andy, to show the finished job. It will be noticed that amongst other things a canopy has been fitted. The control lever for the power steering can be seen in the crewman's hand; manual override is possible through the wheels at either side. It will also be noticed that these rollers can be driven equally well in either direction.*

38. *Burrell Scenic Showman's Road Locomotive No. 4030 'Dolphin' travels from the rally field to the town of Bishop's Castle to take part in the evening's celebrations. Supplied originally to the Staffordshire showman, William Davies, this fine 8NHP engine was the last built at the St. Nicholas works in Thetford; the final Burrell Showman's was No. 4092 'Simplicity' built by Garretts of Leiston in 1930, five years after 'Dolphin' left Thetford. Though not visible here, 'Dolphin' has fittings at the rear for a crane used to assemble heavy rides. A second 'exciter' dynamo is fitted to boost the main unit when starting the ride; the pulley for this 'exciter' can be seen above the offside front wheel.*

39. *I could not resist photographing this meeting between 'King George VI' and Queen Victoria on College Green in the Centre of Bristol. The Queen seems suitably unamused by the passing of John Wharton's 1913 6NHP engine. Occasionally one 'sees' a picture before it is taken; this was one of those occasions and I ran ahead to reach Her Majesty before the Burrell!*

40. 'Princess Mary' - Burrell No. 3949 - is no stranger to latter day road work; indeed in 1988 with regular driver Jim Marsh in charge, she took part in the London to Brighton Run, hauling authentic fairground loads lent by the Harris Family from Sussex. Originally owned by William Nicholls of Forest Gate, the 1925 8NHP compound is seen in Cornwall, with Jim Marsh at her controls.

41. One of the most interesting events involving a showman's engine in 1990 occurred on August 12 at the start of the Paignton Regatta Fair in South Devon. Burrell 8NHP Locomotive No. 3912 'Dragon', built in 1921, joined up with the fair of her original owners - Anderton and Rowland - for the first time since 1939. Following the Torrington Town Band, she led a procession to the fairground hauling the Dodgem Truck from the company's Number two Section; at the fair she also joined up with Anderton's fine Gavioli Organ.

42. *Most survivors of the wagons built by Fodens Ltd at their Sandbach works are 'overtypes' - they have horizontal locomotive type boilers, and open motion and crankshaft above the boiler. A fine example is John Crawley's 1926 built six ton wagon, No. 12364, seen here during a Bristol Run. The 1930 Transport Act penalised wagons with steel or solid rubber tyres, and many, like this one were converted to pneumatics. No. 12364 spent much of its life as a tar sprayer.*

43. *In December 1990, and newly restored, 'King William', Gerald Stoneman's 1926 six ton wagon steams along East Devon's Culm Valley, to Coldharbour Mill. The Mill's 300HP Pollitt and Wigzell 1910 cross compound steam engine and boiler were back in action, their restoration also completed by Gerald and his team. The Mill - a working woollen mill museum - is well worth a visit.*

44/45 *Gerry Stoneman purchased Foden No. 12388 at the much publicised auction at the premises of W G King in Bishop's Lydeard in May 1988. Three traction engines and nine very derelict Foden wagons were sold, in various states of decrepitude. No. 12388 is the first of the nine to be restored having lain out of use since 1930. I have included here two contrasting views which illustrate graphically the achievement of this wagon's restorers in just two and a half years. The upper photograph taken just before the sale, shows No. 12388, complete with sawn off tree stump wedged in her front axle. below she is posed outside the Museum at Coldharbour Mill, with most of the restoration done; the wooden wagon body was yet to be fitted at this stage.*

46.   Another beautifully restored Foden overtype wagon is No. 13316, built in 1929 and restored and rallied by the Horrell Brothers from Stoke Canon near Exeter. Beneath the cover on the back lurks a tanker body, lettered 'Horrells Cider' - a legend which prompts many questions regarding its content!   The chain drive to the rear wheels is clearly seen in this view, as are the boiler, firebox and 'overtype' motion atop the boiler.   No. 13316 was photographed returning home from a Somerset Rally in 1986.

47. In contrast, here we have a product of the Sentinel waggon works in Shrewsbury. Like the Foden above, this model is chain driven, but differs in that it has a vertical boiler and firebox in the cab, and an enclosed engine below the frames behind. The original design was the 'Standard' followed by the 'Super' of which No. 5665, illustrated here is finely restored example built in 1924.

48. Foden wagons also appeared in shorter tractor form and as such were popular with timber hauliers; they were often with a winch for the purpose. No. 10694 built in 1923 has both oil and electric lighting and is clearly steaming well, just beginning to blow off from the safety valves behind the chimney. Noticeable on this tractor, and on wagon No. 12388 are the very distinctive pattern of cast wheels fitted to Foden wagons.

49. The final development of Sentinel waggon was the S4 - the 'S' referring to the fact that they were shaft driven in the manner of a modern truck. Built in four, six and even eight wheel versions, they were fast, economical vehicles, well able to compete with internal combustion units of the day. No. 9032 was built in 1934 and its styling was in many ways ahead of its time; power was provided by a hopper fed vertical boiler in the cab, and an enclosed four cylinder engine. This fine example began its working life in Scotland, but has been owned for many years by Sentinel restorers John and Vincent Goold of Camerton.

50. 'The fairest and most beautiful church in all my realm' - so said Good Queen Bess of St. Mary Redcliffe Church in Bristol, seen hazily behind these two Aveling rollers cautiously descending Redcliff Hill. No. 8196 of 1914 and 10594 of 1923, both ten tonners, are about to turn right at a roundabout; they are not actually overtaking the cars on the right!!

51. *Hand signals may be rare for the modern motorist, but they are very necessary for the driver of a steam engine! Here the driver of a very handsome Burrell traction engine makes his intentions clear as he prepares to make a right turn off the main road. 'Beaver' is an 8NHP single cylinder engine, built in 1897 as No. 2051. Apart from the addition of rubber tyres, she looks much as she would have done when new.*

52. *Also about to turn right is a 1922 Aveling and Porter 8 ton compound convertible roller, No. 9264, 'Lady Hesketh'. Supplied originally, in tractor form to Aberystwyth RDC in West Wales. she later passed to Cardiganshire County Council, spending most of her life in roller form - as beautifully restored by Steve and Rosemary Milns of Ellesmere.*

53. One of the most popular designs marketed by Richard Garrett and Sons of Leiston was their pretty little '4CD' 5 ton tractor. Used by hauliers timber merchants and showman, many ended their lives threshing. No. 33278 'Princess Mary' was new to the War Department in 1918, then spent some time in showland before reverting to haulage form. Owner Nick Baker seems concerned as to the whereabouts of other participants of a road run in Bishop's Lydeard, Somerset!

54. Here we have a well restored example of a Garrett 4CD Showman's Tractor. No. 33566 'Little Billy' was built in 1919, and went to the well known West Country showmen W Cole and Sons of Bristol. Used until 1939 and retained by the Cole family until 1972, it was then sold to Robert Finbow who now keeps it at his 'Mechanical Organ Museum' near Stowmarket. It is seen on a visit to its old haunts for the 1986 Bristol Docks Rally.

55. *Another Garrett 4CD which spent its working life on the fairgrounds is No. 32112 'The Greyhound'. Used originally by the Beach family, it is seen here making rapid progress at the 1990 St. Agnes Rally, with an unusual traction wagon behind.*

56. *Not long after he acquired Garrett No. 31193, Cyril Finch decided to make a midwinter run to a local hostelry. The surroundings and lack of traffic hardly suggest that this photograph was taken in early December of 1987. No. 31193 was built in 1913 as a road roller for Shropshire County Council and was restored as a showmans tractor in 1968. During preservation it has been known as 'Henrietta' (with Henry Fry); 'Yeovil Town' (Alan Fry) and 'Pride of the Valley' (Cyril Finch)!*

57. Occasionally traction engines may appear at local carnivals; a feature of such events in Somerset and Dorset is that some take place in the autumn months, after dark. The 1990 Carnival at Gillingham in Dorset coincided with a local engine owners' reunion, and a number of steamers appeared in the parade. Here Brian and Maria Casely take their beautiful 6NHP Burrell Road Locomotive, No. 3824, 'Lord Fisher of Lambeth' through the streets of Gillingham. Built in December 1919, 'Lord Fisher' worked for Alfred Shire of Thurlbear near Taunton; the engine was running without a canopy, pending construction of a replacement.